Crazy for Ponies

Karen Briggs
and
Shawn Hamilton

Scholastic Canada Ltd.

New York Toronto London Auckland Sydney
Mexico City New Delhi Hong Kong Buenos Aires

Scholastic Canada Ltd.
175 Hillmount Road, Markham, Ontario, L6C 1Z7 Canada

Scholastic Inc.
555 Broadway, New York, NY 10012, USA

Scholastic Australia Pty Limited
PO Box 579, Gosford, NSW 2250, Australia

Scholastic New Zealand Limited
Private Bag 94407, Greenmount, Auckland, New Zealand

Scholastic Publications Ltd.
Villiers House, Clarendon Avenue, Leamington Spa, Warwickshire CV32 5PR, UK

Photos pages 30-31: Karen Briggs; photo page 36 (lower): John F. Mailer,
National Archives of Canada PA-116676.

National Library of Canada Cataloguing in Publication Data

Briggs, Karen, 1963-
Crazy for ponies

ISBN 0-439-98929-9

1. Ponies–Juvenile literature. I. Hamilton, Shawn, 1961- II. Title.

SF315.B75 2002   j363.1'6   C2002-900296-6

6 5 4 3 2 1   Printed in Canada   02 03 04 05 06

A Day in the Life of a Show Pony

Everyone gets up early on the day of the horse show. There's plenty to do, even before the sun comes up! Ponies get bathed  so they're sparkling clean, their manes and tails get braided, and the truck and horse trailer are loaded up with clothes, saddles and supplies. Then the ponies step up into the trailer, where a net full of hay awaits them. They munch their breakfast while being driven to the show grounds.

At a horse show, ponies and riders get to show off the skills they've been practising — but this time they'll do it in front of a judge. Ribbons are awarded for the best performances: a red ribbon for first place in Canada, a blue ribbon in the United States. Sometimes there are trophies and prizes too!

There are many different classes for kids and ponies to enter. Some are equitation classes, which judge the rider's position and skills in piloting her pony. Others are performance classes, where the looks, movement and talents of the pony are judged. Young riders can compete in jumping, and in fun classes like barrel racing and pole-bending, too.

At the end of the show, ponies walk back onto the horse trailer, and kids and parents pile into the truck for the drive home. It's been a long, tiring day, but fun, too — and there are a couple of brightly coloured ribbons to take home and display proudly!

Facing page: Fell pony

Connemara

The Connemara is the pony who flies through the air with the greatest of ease! He is renowned for his jumping ability, often competing successfully against much taller horses.

Named after a craggy, sparsely populated region in western Ireland, the Connemara is the descendent of ponies first brought to the Emerald Isle by the ancient Celts around 500 B.C. These native ponies were thought to have been joined, many centuries later, by horses that survived the sinking of the Spanish Armada (a great fleet of fighting ships) off the Connemara coast in 1588. These horses mixed with the wild herds, contributing their noble blood and greater size. Today the Connemara is the tallest of the British native pony breeds, often standing 14:2 hands or taller (making them officially horse-sized).

Connemara ponies are not only nimble and athletic, but tough and long-lived too. For centuries Irish farmers have depended on them to put in a long day's work. And they couldn't rest on the weekends

when there was fox-hunting and racing to be done, either. The farmers preferred mares, who could give them a foal every year in addition to doing all this work!

Buckskin and gray are the two most common coat colors of Connemaras, but they can also be chestnut, bay, black or any other solid color. They have a willing disposition, and cover the ground in long, sweeping strides, unlike many other ponies' short, choppy steps. The breed has produced many famous jumpers and three-day-event horses.

PONY FACT

Stroller, a Connemara/Thoroughbred cross, is the only pony ever to have competed in the Olympic Games. He won a silver medal in show-jumping at the 1968 Olympics in Mexico City.

Dales

If you know any stories by veterinarian James Herriot, who wrote *All Creatures Great and Small,* you have heard of the wild and remote Yorkshire Dales country in England. This region is the home of the Dales pony, one of nine British native pony breeds. Like the people of Yorkshire, the Dales ponies are hard workers.

Originally they helped to bring lead from the mines in the region, over the hills to the port cities 400 kilometers (250 miles) away. Carrying loads as heavy as 100 kilograms (220 pounds) of lead, ore and fuel, they were tied together in "pack strings" of up to twenty ponies each, led by one rider. They would travel as far as 80 kilometers (50 miles) a day. Then, when they reached the shore, their packs were removed — only to be replaced by a heavy load of coal for the journey home! It's no wonder the Dales ponies gained a reputation for sure-footedness, strength and great endurance.

Because Yorkshire folks also loved to have trotting races, they bred their ponies to have flashy action and speed at the trot. Today, Dales ponies still make wonderful driving ponies, who always look smart hitched to a gleaming little carriage.

Dales ponies come in several solid colors, including black, bay, brown and gray, with only small white markings. They have round compact bodies, and especially hard, tough feet, with long, silky "feathers" just above their hoofs. They are known for their calm yet cheeky personalities!

PONY FACT One farmer loved his Dales pony too much to see him drafted for use by the British Army in the First World War, so he hid him in the kitchen while an army captain waited in the front room!

Exmoor

Exmoor in southwest England is cold, windy and wet. It's an open plain (or moor) of heather and other tough-to-chew plants. Only a very tough little pony with a weatherproof coat could survive here — the Exmoor!

Unlike most horses and ponies, Exmoor ponies grow a double-layered winter coat, which keeps them warm and dry even when the weather is miserable. Their tails come with a "snow-chute" — a patch of short, coarse hairs at the top — which channels rain and snow away from their bodies. And they have a heavy upper eyebrow to help protect their eyes from wind and driving rain. The Exmoors' golden bay color helps them blend into the moors and hide from predators. You can recognize them by the oatmeal-colored ring around their eyes, and the same color on their muzzles — sometimes even on their tummies.

Exmoors can survive on very poor grazing. They are quite small, standing no more than 12:3 hands. But don't let their small size fool you. They are amazingly strong, and can easily carry an adult rider. In fact, they are sometimes thought to be best suited for grown-ups, because they have such a cheeky temperament!

Scientists who study fossil records believe that the Exmoor is one of the most primitive pony breeds on earth, little changed since prehistoric times. When scientists compare recent Exmoor pony skeletons with those of ponies who lived 12,000 years ago in the Exmoor region, the skeletons look very much the same.

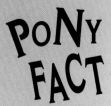

Exmoors were nearly wiped out during the Second World War. Even now there are only about 1200 of them left in the world — making them rarer than China's giant pandas!

Hackney

There is no pony that's fancier or higher-stepping than the proud little Hackney from England — a driving and show pony supreme. He's a pony-sized version of the Hackney horse, a popular and stylish carriage horse during the 18th and 19th centuries.

In the 1880s a man named Christopher Wilson bred his small Hackney stallion, Sir George, to Welsh pony mares. Soon he had a number of foals who had all the flash and quickness of the Hackney horse — in a pint-sized package. Today Hackney horses are rare, but Hackney ponies are popular and thriving!

The word "hackney" used to describe a horse or a carriage that you could rent to take you somewhere, just like the taxis of today. A Hackney pony can still deliver you in style, especially if you want to be in the show ring with all eyes on you and your carriage! He snaps his knees right up under his chin, and his hind feet up to his belly, with each trotting step. His hoofs beat such a quick rhythm that he seems turbo-charged.

Today's Hackney ponies are rarely ridden, though many are remarkable jumpers. Since their temperaments can be excitable, they are not always suitable mounts for young riders, yet they are too small for most adults to ride. It is in harness that they really show off their talents.

PONY FACT

Some Hackneys are shown as "roadsters." They pull carriages around the ring at such high speeds, the carriages skid in all the corners!

Haflinger

As rugged and beautiful as the mountainous Alps that are his home, the golden Haflinger is the pride of Austria. He is an all-around working pony, built like a miniature draft horse, and strong enough to carry or pull a heavy load up and down steep, rocky trails.

The Haflinger's origins can be traced back to medieval times, when many of the mountain villages in Austria and northern Italy could be reached only by narrow paths. A good Haflinger pony was essential to each family in those days, for he was the only reliable form of transportation. When you're traveling on a steep mountain path, you want to make sure that your pony is very sure-footed!

The mountain people also preferred ponies to horses because they were inexpensive to keep, often surviving just on the plants they found growing on the hillsides.

The Haflinger is not only a cheerful, hard worker, he's good-looking too.

All Haflingers are shades of chestnut, ranging from light blond, to the copper of a new penny, to almost chocolate-colored. Their manes and tails are white or cream.

Though their bodies are stocky, their heads are elegant and refined. That comes from the influence of Arabian blood in their past.

Haflingers stand between 13:2 hands and 14:3 hands, and today they are most popular as driving ponies. Because they are so strong, though, they are also wonderful riding ponies for children, or even for adults.

PONY FACT

During the Second World War, hundreds of Haflingers were used by military forces to pack supplies and pull heavy weapons into remote war zones.

Lac La Croix

The rarest and most mysterious pony in Canada is the Lac La Croix, descended from ponies bred on Ojibwa and Mohawk reservation lands over a hundred years ago. It is believed that the blood of both the Canadian horse and the Spanish mustang flow through its veins.

A historian once wrote about large herds of Lac La Croix ponies running free on the banks of the Grand River, in what is now Ontario. He described them as resembling the sturdy black Canadian horse, but in miniature. The ponies were common in Quebec and in the midwestern United States. But for some reason, by the 1970s they were almost extinct. Only four mares remained, living near Lac La Croix in northwestern Ontario, on an isolated Chippewa reserve.

For many years the ponies had spent their summers on an island in the lake, called Pony Island. In the winter they were herded over the ice to be used for logging and other tasks, until the ice was almost ready to melt in the spring. But as the herd had dwindled, and the last stallion was accidentally shot by a hunter, they were left to run wild. When the last four mares were rescued in 1977, they had not felt the touch of a human for almost 10 years, yet the ponies remained gentle to handle.

Because there were no purebred Lac La Croix stallions left, the four mares were bred to a handsome Spanish mustang. Since then a number of foals have been born. There are now about 50 Lac La Croix ponies in Canada and the United States — still very few, but enough to ensure that they will live on and prosper.

PONY FACT Lac La Croix ponies have thick, wavy manes and tails, iron-hard legs and hoofs, and a proud way of carrying themselves. They average about 13:2 hands, and are very curious!

New Forest

The traditional hunting ground of British kings and queens was the New Forest area in the south of England, a land of woodlands, heaths and marshes. This is also the domain of the New Forest pony, who has lived there for centuries.

Many believe that the New Forest pony has been influenced by many non-pony breeds over the centuries, such as the Arabian and also the Thoroughbred. That would account for why he is narrower in build and swifter of foot than many of the other British native ponies. It is only since the 1930s that breeders have concentrated on producing purebred New Forest ponies.

Many of these ponies still wander the vast territory of the New Forest, living like wild horses, although they show little fear of humans. Sometimes they come out of the woods to wander the streets of the villages in the area. In the autumn they love to eat the acorns that fall from the trees. When they eat a lot of them, they sometimes act a little drunk!

Once a year the ponies are rounded up and inspected by the New Forest Pony Breeding and Cattle Society. The ponies with the best conformation (build) and temperaments are chosen to be used for breeding, and their foals are popular as riding ponies. Clever and quick, New Forest ponies are particularly good at jumping. They're also used for pony races, which are a long-standing tradition in the area.

PONY FACT

Although these ponies look wild, they are not. The owners mark their ponies by trimming the tail in a special way. This helps in identifying the ponies from a distance.

British Riding Pony

In the 1800s, when the British Empire ruled India, polo was a favorite pastime. But polo demands a very talented pony. A good polo pony is small and swift, can turn on a dime, and has the energy and heart to keep galloping after the ball, even when he is tired.

The British Army officers found that the best polo mounts were a mixture of Thoroughbred and Arabian blood, with perhaps a little Welsh or Connemara pony blood added. They founded the British Polo and Riding Pony Society in 1893 to register and keep track of the best ponies. When the officers returned to England, they often brought their most prized polo mounts with them.

Gradually, polo players began to prefer a larger horse for playing the game. But people still admired the elegant looks and speed of the ponies, so they decided to breed them for British children to ride and show. Today's British Riding Pony has the look of a miniature Thoroughbred racehorse, but he also has the clever nature of a pony. He is not as hardy as a British native pony such as an Exmoor or a New Forest, and needs to be pampered a bit, with more feed and a warm blanket in the winter. He is a little excitable in temperament, and has beauty, speed and jumping ability.

In England, British Riding Ponies are very popular in the show ring. So far, there are only a few of these ponies in North America, but with looks like these, they are sure to attract attention!

PONY FACT

Each polo team has four players and ponies. A period of play is called a "chukker," and it lasts for eight minutes. Most polo players keep at least two ponies at the ready so that one can rest while the other one plays.

Norwegian Fjord

Many thousands of years ago, during the last Ice Age, people spent the long winter nights huddled in caves. Some of them drew pictures on the cave walls, and horses were one of their favorite subjects. Today we can look at the cave drawings left by these primitive peoples and notice right away that the horses look like Norwegian Fjords.

The Norwegian Fjord pony is named after the narrow, finger-like channels, or *fjords* (fee-ORDS) on the coastline of his native Norway. Even though he is small, he is very strong. He was once the war horse of the Vikings, and a valued possession. In fact, war horses were prized so highly that when a Viking warrior died, his horse was often buried with him, in the belief that it would carry him in the next life.

Norwegian Fjords have not changed much since those days. They are still dun in color (ranging from a pale cream shade to the color of honey) with a dark stripe down their spines and faint zebra-stripe markings on their legs. Like their relatives, the Haflingers, they are built like small, stocky draft horses — but they have a mane that is unique to them. It is dark in the center, with white hairs on either side. Fjord owners trim it in a traditional crescent shape so that it stands upright. The dark hairs stand out against the white ones and make the pony look striking indeed!

Norwegian Fjords stand between 13:2 and 15 hands tall and may weigh as much as 500 kilograms (1100 pounds). They are great family horses who can do a little bit of everything, and they are renowned for their gentle temperaments.

PONY FACT The Norwegian Fjord may be related to the Przewalski's Horse (pronounced serve-OW-ski), the only truly wild horse left in the world today.

Pony of the Americas

Many pony breeds have been around for thousands of years. But the Pony of the Americas is almost brand new — and it's a pony designed just for kids.

The history of the Pony of the Americas, or POA, began in 1954 when a beautiful spotted colt was born on Les Boomhower's farm in Iowa. The foal's mother had Arabian and Appaloosa parents, and his father was a Shetland pony. The newborn baby was white, with black markings like paint smears all over his body. On one flank was a marking that looked like a human hand, so he was given the name Black Hand.

Black Hand grew up to be a handsome pony who could do almost anything he was asked to do. He had such a sensible and kind temperament that he could be ridden by children, even though he was a stallion. Mr. Boomhower decided Black Hand would be the perfect sire to help him found a new breed of ponies — ponies just the right size for children to ride on the ranch or in the show ring.

The ponies would combine the best qualities of the Arabian, the Appaloosa and the Shetland. With Black Hand as the foundation stallion, the new breed, named the Pony of the Americas, had pretty "dished" faces, sturdy and well-muscled bodies, and flashy spotted coats.

POAs must stand 14 hands or less at the withers (shoulders). They are speedy enough for fun games like barrel racing and pole-bending, but quiet enough even for very young riders. These good-looking ponies are winning fans all over the world.

PONY FACT

Like the Appaloosas, POAs have striped hoofs and spotted skin on their muzzles. Their eyes also have a white ring, which makes them look almost human.

Shetland

Small and shaggy he may be, but the Shetland pony has a noble heritage. For many centuries he has been helping humans scrape out a living in the harsh climate of Scotland's Shetland Islands. He has dragged seaweed from the shore to fertilize the stony fields, and carried peat from the bogs and marshes for the family fireplace. The Islanders even used his tail hair to make fishing lines. Some of the earliest known carvings in stone on the Shetland Islands show a man riding a very small pony — a pony that doesn't look very different from the round-bodied little Shetland we love today.

Because the Shetland Islands are

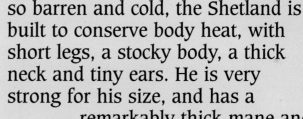

so barren and cold, the Shetland is built to conserve body heat, with short legs, a stocky body, a thick neck and tiny ears. He is very strong for his size, and has a remarkably thick mane and tail, and a heavy, water-repellent winter coat. He survives on the most meager of plants, often adding seaweed to his diet in the winter.

Until the 1970s Shetlands worked underground in mines in Great Britain and Canada. Their small size (less than 10:2 hands) meant that these "pit ponies" could pull loads of coal and ore along the narrow underground shafts where a larger pony could not fit.

The addition of Hackney blood to the Shetland pony has created a second type called the American Shetland. He is very different from the furry British Shetland — sleek, high-stepping and more excitable. He is often used as a driving pony, and is most at home in the show ring. Both types of Shetlands can come in any color, including pinto, and both share an intelligent, curious nature.

PONY FACT

Some people think that the Shetland pony is descended from Icelandic horses brought to the Islands by the Vikings. Icelandics and Shetlands do share many similar coat colors.

Gypsy Vanner

In Ireland and the United Kingdom, there were always traveling tradespeople who went from village to village in brightly painted, horse-drawn caravans that were both their home and their transportation. Called Gypsies or Romanies because of their Romanian heritage, these wanderers seldom stayed in one place for very long, so they depended on their ponies every day. They wanted a pony who was strong, trustworthy, gentle — and eye-catching too!

The Gypsy Vanner is the pony for the job. He is really a cob — a large pony or small horse who has draft horse characteristics and is useful for both driving and riding.

Gypsy Vanners stand between 14 and 15:2 hands, and have long, thick manes and tails, and flashy "feathers" around their hoofs. They come in all sorts of colors, but the most prized are the splashy pintos, especially the black-and-white ones called piebalds. Imagine a jaunty piebald pony, hitched to a red and green caravan — they must have made a cheerful sight in the Irish countryside!

Clydesdales, Shires, Friesians and Dales ponies have all lent their fine qualities to the Gypsy Vanner, which is now a recognized breed. In 1996 the first Gypsy Vanners were imported to North America, where they are fast becoming popular as driving horses. But many are still found in the British Isles, and some are still at work pulling pretty caravans for the Romany folk who follow the old ways of traveling the back roads, as they have for hundreds of years.

PONY FACT

The Gypsy Vanner goes by many different names, including Gypsy Cob, Romany Cob and Irish Tinker pony. (A tinker is a person who does metal work, and repairs pots and pans.)

Trottingbred

When you think of the thrilling sport of harness racing, you usually think of Standardbreds. But ponies race in harness too!

The Trottingbred pony was developed in the 1950s by breeding small Standardbreds to Welsh, Hackney and Shetland ponies. He's a harness-racing specialist who races both at the trot and at the pace. Speedy and competitive, the Trottingbred pony makes going to the races a fun family event. In the eastern United States and in Canada, as well as in Italy, Australia and on the island of Bermuda, these ponies are often owned and raced by kids!

If you go to a pony race, you'll see that Trottingbreds wear the same sort of harness as full-sized Standardbreds. They pull a slightly smaller version of the Standardbred two-wheeled sulky, or race bike. Trottingbreds race a distance of about three-quarters of a kilometer (half a mile), and are ranked according to how fast they have gone in speed trials. That way, ponies of the same ability race against each other. Mares, geldings and stallions all race together, and sometimes there are both trotters and pacers in a single race too. Pacers tend to be a little faster, but the trotters have a surprising home-stretch kick!

Trottingbred ponies come in every color, including pinto, palomino, roan and a beautiful liver chestnut shade with a flaxen mane and tail. They have to be no bigger than 12:2 hands for racing, but some that grow larger make good mounts for experienced young riders.

PONY FACT

Many Trottingbred ponies keep racing right into their late teen years — long after most other kinds of racehorses have retired.

Welsh

The Welsh pony, hailing from the rugged hills of Wales in Great Britain, may be the prettiest and most popular pony in the world. His elegantly dished face, little fox ears and nimble movement have won him fans wherever he goes!

There are four different types of Welsh ponies. The Welsh Mountain pony, or Section A Welsh, is considered the oldest type. He is also the smallest, standing just 12 hands or less. Charming and delicate-looking, he is surprisingly strong, and makes a good beginner's pony for a young child, or a driving pony for an adult.

The Welsh pony (Section B) is a slightly larger version, standing up to 13:2 hands. The extra height was achieved by breeding Welsh Mountain ponies with a couple of carefully selected Thoroughbred and Hackney horse stallions, back in the 1800s. Section B Welsh ponies are clever jumpers and are very popular for older children.

The Welsh Pony of Cob Type (Section C) also has a height limit of 13:2 hands, but is a heavier, stockier pony than the Section B. Before the time of cars, country doctors in England used to depend on him to speed them between appointments.

The Welsh Cob (Section D) is a horse-sized version of the Welsh pony. He's sturdy, broad and a high-stepper, showing the influence of noble Spanish blood somewhere in his past. He has true pony intelligence and character, but in a bigger package.

All Welsh ponies are energetic but sensible, and very athletic — with forceful, ground-covering strides. They have large luminous eyes, an Arabian-type dished face, and may be any solid color, though grays are common.

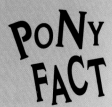

PONY FACT When a knight in the Middle Ages led his war horses into battle, he would ride his Welsh Cob so that the war horses would be fresh and ready when they were needed.

Fell

Born and bred in the north of England, among the hills, or "fells," the Fell pony is dark and handsome. He can trace his ancestry all the way back to horses brought to the British Isles by the invading Romans in 55 B.C. His history was also shaped by the Vikings and the Normans, who conquered England in the centuries after the Roman Empire collapsed. Through all of these changes the Fell pony has survived, thanks to his toughness and his helpful nature.

The Fell is closely related to the Dales pony, but he is somewhat larger because of early cross-breeding with the Friesian, an elegant black carriage horse. A little Clydesdale blood was also brought in about a century ago. As a result, the Fell pony resembles a small Friesian, with snappy knee action at the trot and a proud, high-headed bearing.

The Fell pony has been a jack-of-all-trades over the centuries. He has been used to pack lead ore from the mines to the seaports, and to help the Normans herd their sheep and plow their land. He might even have hauled stones for the building of the Roman walls that still dot the British landscape.

Today he's much in demand as a driving pony, and is also popular for pony-trekking, where his sure-footedness and ability to carry weight make him suitable for even tall grown-ups. He is not speedy, but he can work for many hours without tiring.

Most Fell ponies are solid black, though there are a few who are bay or gray. They sport a thick, flowing mane and tail, tough hoofs that are so black they almost look blue, and "feathering" around the feet. They stand between 13 and 14 hands tall.

PONY FACT

England's Queen Elizabeth II is a fan of Fell ponies. She keeps several at her estate in Balmoral, in Scotland.

34

See page 3 for full-page photo of the Fell pony.

Chincoteague

The Chincoteague pony (pronounced SHIN-co-teeg) is one of the most famous pony breeds in the world. That's because a Chincoteague mare starred in one of the best-known children's books about horses, Marguerite Henry's *Misty of Chincoteague.*

The ponies live wild on the sandbar island of Assateague off the coast of the eastern United States. No one is quite sure how they first arrived there. One story is that they survived the shipwreck of a Spanish galleon in the 16th century. It's more likely that they were turned loose on the island in the 1700s by farmers who didn't want to pay taxes for owning horses!

The horses soon adapted to life without human help, but they had to learn to eat the tough, salty sea-grasses that grow on the sand dunes, to dig with their hoofs for fresh water to drink, and to hide among the trees when storms swept

in from the Atlantic Ocean. In the summer, when the biting flies are fierce, they found relief by standing neck-deep in the surf. The harsh conditions stunted their growth, so that over time the surviving horses were all pony-sized, as they remain today.

Because Assateague Island is so small, it can support only a limited number of ponies. On Pony Penning Day each year, the ponies are herded into the water at low tide, and they swim across the channel to Chincoteague Island. There, the foals are sold at an auction and go on to become riding ponies. The older ponies are swum back across the channel after the auction, to live in peace until the next year.

PONY FACT

Chincoteague ponies are protected by law. You can see the ponies, but not touch them, if you visit the Chincoteague National Wildlife Reserve or the Assateague Island National Seashore.

See center spread for photo of the Chincoteague pony.

Ponies with Jobs

Ponies are cute, and ponies are cuddly, but they're a lot more than just pets! Some ponies work hard to help people, just like their bigger cousins, the horses. Here are just some of the jobs ponies can do.

Weight-pulling

Through much of their history, ponies have been used to help carry or pull loads. Today some ponies compete in "pony pulls." The ponies are hitched to a stone boat — a slab of concrete on rails, sometimes weighing over 100 kilograms (over 200 pounds). When the judge says "Go!" the ponies dig in and pull as hard as they can! The winners are those that pull the heaviest weight a certain distance.

Pit Ponies

For many years, pit ponies helped people by working underground in mines. They were small enough to work in the mines' low tunnels and help carry the coal and ore that would then be taken to the surface. Though they were usually well-cared for, it was a hard life. Sometimes the ponies didn't see the light of day for years at a time. Only when they retired did they have the pleasure of grazing in a grassy field again.

Therapeutic Ponies

Riding is wonderful exercise for people with physical injuries or handicaps. Imagine having to use a wheelchair to get around — on a pony you would have a freedom you'd never felt before! There are therapeutic riding programs all over the world, for kids and grown-ups with mental or physical disabilities. A therapeutic riding pony is a very special animal — he has to be steady, reliable and very, very patient and kind. Many are older ponies who are almost ready to retire. But they still enjoy being helpful, and they are much loved by the lucky people who ride them.

Riding School Ponies

Ponies who work in riding schools have to be very well-trained and patient. They might be ridden by many different people every week — some of them beginners, some of them more experienced riders. Although there is always a riding instructor in the ring to help the students, a good school pony is like a teacher too. They are not always the most glamorous ponies, but their experience and wisdom make them worth their weight in gold.

BRITISH RIDING PONY
The National Pony Society
Willingdon House
102 High Street
Alton, Hampshire
GU34 1EN
United Kingdom

CHINCOTEAGUE PONY
Chincoteague Pony Association
P.O. Box 407
Chincoteague, Virginia
USA 23336-0407

The National Chincoteague
  Pony Association
c/o Gale Park Frederick
2595 Jensen Road
Bellingham, Washington
USA 98226

CONNEMARA PONY
English Connemara Pony
  Society
Glen Fern
Waddicombe, Dulverton
Somerset TA22 9RY
United Kingdom

American Connemara Pony
  Society
2360 Hunting Ridge Road
Winchester, Virginia
USA 22603

DALES PONY
The Dales Pony Society of
  America Inc.
261 River Street
Halifax, Massachusetts
USA 02338

Dales Pony Association of
  North America
P.O. Box 733
Walkerton, Ontario
Canada N0G 2V0

EXMOOR PONY
The Exmoor Pony Society
Glen Fern
Waddicombe, Dulverton
Somerset TA22 9RY
United Kingdom

North American Exmoors
c/o Anne Holmes
P.O. Box 155
Ripley, Ontario
Canada N0G 2R0

FELL PONY
The Fell Pony Society
Federation House
Gilwilly Industrial Estate
Penrith
Cumbria CA11 9BL
United Kingdom

GYPSY VANNER
The Gypsy Vanner Horse
  Society
PO Box 771077
Ocala, Florida
USA 34477-1077

HACKNEY PONY
Canadian Hackney Society
7737 Dalmony Road
Osgoode, Ontario
Canada K0A 2W0

HAFLINGER PONY
American Haflinger Registry
2746 State Route 44
Rootstown, Ohio
USA 44272

LAC LA CROIX PONY
The Lac Lac Croix Pony
c/o Environmental and
  Resource Studies Program
Trent University
1600 West Bank Drive
Peterborough, Ontario
Canada K9J 7B8

NEW FOREST PONY
New Forest Pony Association
  and Registry
PO Box 206
Pascoag, Rhode Island
USA 02859

NORWEGIAN FJORD
Canadian Fjord Horse
  Association
PO Box 1335
Killarney, Manitoba
Canada R0K 1G0

Norwegian Fjord Horse
  Registry
1203 Appian Drive
Webster, New York
USA 14580

PONY OF THE AMERICAS
Pony of the Americas Club, Inc.
5240 Elmwood Avenue
Indianapolis, Indiana
USA 46203

**SHETLAND &
  AMERICAN SHETLAND**
Canadian Pony Society
RR #1
Jarvis, Ontario
Canada N0A 1J0

American Shetland Pony Club
81B East Queenwood
Morton, Illinois
USA 61550

TROTTINGBRED PONY
International Trotting and
  Pacing Association
60 Gulf Road
Gouverneur, New York
USA 13642

WELSH PONY & WELSH COB
Welsh Pony and Cob Society of
  Canada
Box 95530, 350 Davis Drive
Newmarket, Ontario
Canada L3Y 8J8

The Welsh Pony and Cob
  Society of America
PO Box 2977
Winchester, Virginia
USA 22604-2977

Australian Pony Club Council Inc.
P.O. Box 46
Lockhart, New South Wales
2656 Australia

Pony Club Association of NSW
PO Box 980
Glebe, New South Wales
2037 Australia

Pony Club Association of
  Queensland
PO Box 2378
Fortitude Valley, Queensland
4006 Australia

Pony Club Association of South
  Australia
Room 5 — 1st floor
1 Sturt Street
Adelaide, South Australia
5000 Australia

Pony Club Association of
  Victoria
Irving House
12 Warleigh Grove
North Brighton, Victoria
3186 Australia

*This book is dedicated, with love,
to the memory of Pokey — my teacher,
confidant, and partner in crime for
22 years. Thank you for every moment.*
— Karen

*To Pokey, for the adventurous and
invigorating rides, but also for your
patience and kindness in teaching
my daughter, Nicky.*

— Shawn